BOOKWORMS

Nature's Formations

How Are Rivers Formed?

B.J. Best

Cavendish Square
New York

Published in 2018 by Cavendish Square Publishing, LLC
243 5th Avenue, Suite 136, New York, NY 10016

First Edition

Library of Congress Cataloging-in-Publication Data

Names: Best, B.J.
Title: How are rivers formed? / B.J. Best.
Description: New York : Cavendish Square Publishing, 2018. | Series: Nature's formations | Includes index.
Identifiers: ISBN 9781502625410 (pbk.) | ISBN 9781502625434 (library bound) | ISBN 9781502625427 (6 pack) | ISBN 9781502625441 (ebook)
Subjects: LCSH: Rivers--Juvenile literature.
Classification: LCC GB1203.8 B47 2018 | DDC 551.48'3--dc23

Editorial Director: David McNamara
Copy Editor: Nathan Heidelberger
Associate Art Director: Amy Greenan
Designer: Alan Sliwinski
Production Coordinator: Karol Szymczuk
Photo Research: J8 Media

The photographs in this book are used by permission and through the courtesy of: Cover Saara Ansari/Moment/Getty Images; p. 5 ChucknGale Robbins/iStock/Thinkstock; p. 7 Ed Z/Shutterstock.com; p. 9 /Patrik Tedrak/iStock/Thinkstock; p. 11 John Brueske/iStock/Thinkstock; p. 13 Anna Jedynak/Shutterstock.com; p. 15 Dimos/iStock/Thinkstock; p. 17 Phatthanit/Shutterstock.com; p. 19 Tanya Snark/iStock/Thinkstock; p. 21 Hans Blossey/Getty Images.

Printed in the United States of America

Contents

How Rivers Are Formed....... **4**

New Words **22**

Index **23**

About the Author............. **24**

Rivers are made of flowing water.

River water comes from many places.

It comes from rain.

It comes from melting snow.

River water can come
from lakes.

It can come
from underground.

It comes up from **springs**.

Water always flows downhill.

Water goes to the lowest place on land.

A river begins as a bit of flowing water.

Small rivers can be called streams.

They can be called **creeks**.

Water can cut away land.

A river makes a **channel**.

The channel is the
river's path.

Banks are the sides of a river.

They are higher than the water.

They keep the river in its channel.

Rivers get bigger as they get longer.

They get more water.

Rivers can join together.

This will also make a bigger river.

The **mouth** is the end of the river.

Most river water ends up in an ocean.

The water is done flowing!

New Words

banks (BANX) The sides of a river.

channel (CHA-nul) A river's path.

creeks (CREEKS) Small rivers.

mouth (MOWTH) The end of a river.

springs (SPRINGZ) Places where water comes up from underground.

Index

banks, 16

channel, 14, 16

creeks, 12

flowing, 4, 10, 20

melting, 6

mouth, 20

springs, 8

streams, 12

About the Author

B.J. Best lives in Wisconsin with his wife and son. He has written many other books for children. He has kayaked on the Mississippi River.

About BOOKWORMS

Bookworms help independent readers gain reading confidence through high-frequency words, simple sentences, and strong picture/text support. Each book explores a concept that helps children relate what they read to the world they live in.